Growing up in
JUDAISM

Jean Holm

Series editor: Jean Holm

What is this book about?

One of the most interesting ways to learn about a religion is to try to see it through the eyes of children who are growing up in a religious family. In this way we can discover something of what it *feels* like to belong to the religion.

In the books in this series we shall be finding out how children gradually come to understand the real meaning of the festivals they celebrate, the scriptures and other stories they hear, the ceremonies they take part in, the symbols of their religion and the customs and traditions of their religious community. This should provide a good foundation for going on to a wider study of the religions.

The five books in this series deal with the main religions that are found in Britain today: Christianity, Hinduism, Islam, Judaism and Sikhism. However, some things are more important in one religion than in another. For example, festivals play a bigger part in the lives of Jewish children than they do in the lives of Sikh children, and the scriptures play a bigger part in the lives of Muslim children than they do in the lives of Hindu children, so although many of the same topics are dealt with in all the books, the pattern of each book is slightly different.

There are differences within every religion as well as between religions, and even a very long book could not describe the customs and beliefs of all the groups that make up a religion. In these books we may be learning more about one of the groups, or traditions, within the religion, but there will be references to the different ways in which other groups practise their faith.

In this series of books we are using BCE (Before the Christian Era) and CE (in the Christian Era) instead of BC and AD, which refer to Christian beliefs about the significance of Jesus.

How to use this book

Some of you will be studying religions for the first time. Others may already have learnt something about places of worship or festivals, and you will be able to gain greater understanding and fit what you know into a wider picture of the religion.

As you learn about how children grow up in a religion, prepare a display, or perhaps make a large class book. You will find some suggestions of activities in the text, but you will be able to think of many more. If your display is good enough it might be possible to put it up in the hall or in a corridor so that lots of people can see it. Try to show what it feels like to be on the 'inside' of the religion, so that other pupils and teachers and visitors to the school will be able to learn about the religion from the point of view of the children who are growing up in it.

Contents

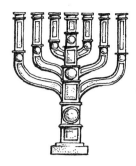

Times and seasons

Shabbat

שַׁבָּת שָׁלוֹם **Shabbat Shalom**

Jewish children have a party every week. There are many festivals in the religion of Judaism, but the most important of them is the one that begins at sunset every Friday — the Sabbath, or to give it its Hebrew name, Shabbat. It is called the queen of the special days, and families prepare for it just as they would if they had a very important guest coming into their home. The house is cleaned, the family put on their best clothes, and especially tasty food is prepared.

At the moment Shabbat begins it is welcomed in by the woman of the house. She lights at least two candles in a ceremony called 'the kindling of the Sabbath lights'. The greeting which people give to each other is 'Shabbat Shalom', which means 'A Good Sabbath' — 'May you have a peaceful Sabbath'.

Jewish people use '**Shalom**'* as a greeting and to say 'good-bye'. It is short for 'Peace be with you'.

For Jewish people the day begins at sunset. In Genesis 1 we read 'Evening came, and morning came, the first day'.

"In the winter you have to leave school early. My dad picks me up. I think the earliest Shabbat will come in this winter is about 3.30, so my dad will pick me up about 3 o'clock. When I get home I get ready and have a shower. You normally have special clothes for Shabbat, and some jewellry or whatever, to make you look nice."

*"Mum lights the candles while we are still at **shul** and that is when Shabbat has started. When I was little I always had my own set of candles, so I learned how to light the candles and welcome in Shabbat."*

---

* The words in the glossary are printed in **bold** type the first time they appear in the book.

Shabbat evening meal

"We have a really nice meal — you get full up! It lasts about an hour. We eat and talk, and we sing zemirot. *I know lots of them. You don't learn them specially. You're used to hearing them, so you just pick them up. My sister is five and she knows one or two."*

Here is part of a zemirah. It refers to an ancient tradition that two angels accompanied a man on his way home from the synagogue at the beginning of the Sabbath. Its title means 'Peace be with you'.

Shalom Aleiḥem

Peace be with you, ministering angels,
    angels of the Most High,
  the supreme King of Kings, the Holy One,
    Blessed be He.

Enter in peace, messengers of peace,
    angels of the Most High,
  the supreme King of Kings, the Holy One,
    Blessed be He.

"Mummy starts getting ready for Shabbat on Thursday. I help her cook ḥallah. *And if she's making salad it's quite easy to help."*

"I'm sure that when our children were small they thought that apple crumble was part of the Shabbat ritual, but the only reason we have it so often is that it is my husband's favourite pudding!"

Hallah is a special kind of bread, made with eggs. There are two ḥallot which symbolise the two portions of manna that the Israelites gathered every Friday when they were living in the wilderness over three thousand years ago. (⟶ Exodus 16)

The blessing over wine — **Kiddush** — is said before the meal. Then after a symbolic washing of hands the family returns to the table and the blessing over bread — **Ha-Motzi** — is said.

> Kiddush: 'Blessed are you, O Lord our God, King of the Universe, who creates the fruit of the vine.'
>
> Ha-Motzi: 'Blessed are you, O Lord our God, King of the Universe, who brings forth bread from the earth.'

A day without work

No one does any work once the festival has begun (and that includes homework), because Shabbat is the festival which honours God as Creator. The Book of Genesis tells how God rested after the six days of creation. So Shabbat is a happy, relaxed day, and the children know that their parents will be free to spend time with them. They can ask questions and talk about what they have been doing during the week.

Shabbat has always been regarded by the Jewish people as a precious gift from God. One of the Rabbis many centurues ago said, 'The Sabbath was given over to man and not man to the Sabbath'.

"You're not supposed to do any work, which means not writing, not going in the car, not riding bikes, not switching on lights. It can be a pain when all your friends are going down town, or you want to be in the netball team. But it's a positive day because you are doing things. It's not boring. It's a great time for meeting people. You've got all day. Sometimes we play games with the whole family together. And friends come round. It's really great."

Because life is sacred in Judaism, any action which helps to save life over-rides all the commands about not working on Shabbat. Jewish doctors and nurses, for example, can continue their work of healing on Shabbat.

"The family tell stories about me when I was small. One of them is about Shabbat. You are not supposed to play musical instruments on Shabbat. I went to the piano and started to play. I was told, 'In this house we don't do that on Shabbat'. Apparently I looked up and said sweetly, 'I do!' I don't remember that so I must have been very little."

"It's called a day of rest. I like to lie in a bit on Saturday morning. Then we go to synagogue. It lasts from 9.30 to 11.30. I don't always go right at the beginning."

Children go to the synagogue with their parents on the morning of Shabbat. This is the most important service of the week (⟶ page 43).

Families

Jewish parents and children feel very close to each other, and one of the ways that this is shown is in the custom of the father blessing his children before the Friday evening meal. He puts his hands on their heads, and says to his sons, 'God make thee as Ephraim and Manasseh', and to his daughters, 'God make thee as Sarah, Rebekah, Rachel and Leah'.

The father's blessing of his son comes from Genesis 48:20. The blessing of his daughter refers to the wives of Abraham, Isaac and Jacob.

"Every week we used to have a sort of ceremony. We still do. After dad has **davened** *— and now, since my Bar Mitzvah, after I have davened too — we all sing Shalom Aleiḥem. And then Dad blesses us, each in turn because there is a different blessing for girls and for boys. He puts his hands on our heads and says the blessing and kisses us on the forehead, and says, 'Shabbat shalom'. Then you know that you can really relax, and Shabbat's in. It's a nice feeling of the family being together, and warmth, and the kind of friendliness and contact with parents that I don't think many of the people at school have, where the parent often seems to be thought of as the 'bad guy'. In Jewish families it's not the case. The parent is supportive, and the 'good guy' really."*

"Ever since I was a child I've looked forward to Shabbat — and I still do. I can't play in school matches, but that is just something I live with. I've never had to think in my mind, which do I choose, Shabbat or other things."

Begin to make a collection of symbols and symbolic actions in Judaism. Beside each one say when it would be used, and what children growing up in Judaism would learn from it. Add to your collection as you go through this book.

Havdalah

Shabbat lasts for about twenty-five hours. It ends at twilight on Saturday with the **Havdalah** ceremony. Havdalah means 'separation', and the ritual of the ceremony helps to express what Shabbat means to Jewish people. The father of the family says four blessings:

The first is said over a cup overflowing with wine, as a symbol of the overflowing joy of Shabbat.

The second is said over a spice box which is passed round for everyone to smell the sweet spices, as a symbol of the fragrance of Shabbat which is to be carried over into the rest of the week.

The third is said over a light as a symbol of the first act of creation, when God said 'Let there be light'.

The fourth blesses God for making a distinction between the seventh day and the six working days.

The family may sing Havdalah songs, ending with Psalm 150.

The first three stars

"We always made Havdalah at the end of Shabbat. We used to look out of the window to see when it was dark. The rule is that Shabbat has ended when you can see three stars. Of course it's usually cloudy in this country so we'd have to go by the book, which gives the exact time. There were three boys in our family, and we always suffered because the tradition is that the youngest girl holds the candle, and the youngest girl in our household was my mother!"

"Even if you haven't made Havdalah, you're allowed to say a shorter prayer about God dividing between holiness and the rest of the week — and then you can switch lights on and write. I go up to my room and open letters which have come."

Here is the special Havdalah prayer:

'Blessed are you, O Lord our God, King of the Universe, who makes a distinction between light and darkness, between the holy and the ordinary, between Israel and the nations, between the Sabbath and the weekday.'

A plaited candle is used for Havdalah. It must have at least two lights.

"Judaism is always presented to children not as a chore but as an enjoyable way of life. There's always something that the child can look forward to. Our parents always involved us from the earliest days — things like washing your hands and having wine with your meal for the Kiddush. It's as soon as you can eat and drink, basically. Even at Havdalah, at the end of Shabbat, when we light the candles. If it was just past our bedtime we'd get changed and get ready for bed and they'd bring us down again for Havdalah. You can say Havdalah to the following Tuesday morning, according to the Law, so in summer, when we couldn't stay up till Shabbat was out, we used to do it on Sunday morning."

Shabbat is so important in Judaism that the other days in the week are thought of in relation to it. The week is divided in two: Wednesday, Thursday and Friday are thought of as related to the Shabbat which is to come, and Sunday, Monday and Tuesday to the Shabbat which has just passed. That is why the Havdalah ceremony can be done at any time up to Tuesday.

If you were spending Shabbat with a Jewish family, what sorts of things would you see and hear and eat? Think of some interesting ways to convey this information to other people.

Meeting Hebrew

Children who live in Israel speak Hebrew, because it is the language of the country. When they are about five years old they learn to write it as well. But many Jewish children who live in other countries learn Hebrew as well as the language of the country. Their Bible is written in Hebrew, and if they belong to the Orthodox movement in Judaism, the prayers are in Hebrew too.

You have already come across several Hebrew words in this book, and you might like to know a little bit more about the language, so that you can recognise the Hebrew letters. You will also want to include some Hebrew if you are preparing a display to show what it is like to grow up in Judaism.

Hebrew is written from right to left. It has no capital letters. There are twenty-two letters in the Hebrew alphabet, but they are all consonants! For many hundreds of years the language was written without any vowels, so it was like writing LSSNS for LESSONS. Later in the book we shall meet the vowels.

Hebrew is written in a different script from European languages, but if we learn to transliterate it – put its letters into English letters – we often find that we know the word. The Hebew letter ש is 'sh', ב is 'bb' and ת is 't'. So the transliteration of שבת is sh-bb-t, though of course when we say the word it is Shabbat.

Before trying the first task below, read the information about the Hebrew alphabet contained in the box on the next page. Hebrew is a difficult language to learn, but the little bit of Herbrew that we shall be doing in this book is really just for fun. Think how hard it must be for Jewish children who have to learn the language properly.

---

1 If you try to put your name into Hebrew letters, don't forget to write from right to left.

2 As you go through this book you might like to build up your own list of Hebrew words, in Hebrew script and in English. When you have a good number of words in your list, decide whether you want to group them under headings, such as festivals, symbols, etc.

The alphabet

LETTER	FINAL FORM	NAME	SOUND	ENGLISH LETTER	The columns show:
א		Alef	silent	ʾ	1 The Hebrew letter.
ב		Bet	b	b	2 How some letters are written when they come at the end of a word.
ב		Bet	v	v	
ג		Gimel	g	g	3 What the letters are called (e.g. as we call 'h', 'aitch').
ד		Dalet	d	d	
ה		Hay	h	h	4 How to pronounce the letters; three of them are pronounced differently when they have a dot in them.
ו		Vav	v	v	
ז		Zayin	z	z	
ח		Ḥet	ch	ḥ	
ט		Tet	t	t	5 Which English letter to use for each Hebrew letter. (Some books use a different system of transliteration, e.g. 'ch' instead of 'ḥ', so Hanukkah would be Chanukkah.)
י		Yod	y	y (or j)	
כ	ך	Kaf	k	k	
כ	ך	Kaf	kh	kh	
ל		Lamed	l	l	
מ	ם	Mem	m	m	A dot in a letter in the middle of a word often shows that the letter is doubled, e.g. שַׁבָּת (Shabbat).
נ	ן	Nun	n	n	
ס		Sameḥ	s	s	Two consonants ו and
ע		Ayin	silent	ʿ	י can represent vowels, Vav represents 'o'
פ	ף	Pay	p	p	in 'shalom' שָׁלוֹם
פ	ף	Pay	f	f	and 'u' in 'kiddush' קִדּוּשׁ
צ	ץ	Tsadi	tz	tz	
ק		Kuf	k	k	
ר		Resh	r	r	
שׁ		Shin	sh	sh	
שׂ		Sin	s	s	
ת		Tav	t	t	

Pesaḥ

*"Pesaḥ is my favourite festival. I like **Seder** night because I can stay up late, to midnight, or 2 o'clock."*

Shabbat is a weekly festival, but there are also a number of annual festivals in Judaism, and in this book we shall be learning about the ones which are especially important to children.

The oldest festival is Pesaḥ, the Feast of Passover. It is a spring festival, but it also celebrates the escape of the Hebrew people from slavery in Egypt more than three thousand years ago. There are so many special things for children to do that it is very easy for them to learn about its meaning. When they are little they enjoy helping to spring-clean the house, and get out the cups, saucers and plates which are kept just for this festival. They watch their mother going through the kitchen cupboards, taking out all the leavened food – food that has a substance in it, like yeast, that makes it rise during cooking. The Hebrew word for leavened food is **ḥametz**. For the seven or eight days of the festival (⟶ page 27) they will eat **matzah**, unleavened bread.

On the day before Pesaḥ starts the children have a 'treasure hunt'. Their parents hide a number of pieces of ḥametz – usually bread – around the house, and the children search for them. There is great excitement when all the pieces have been found, and next morning the bread is ceremonially burnt. So from when they are very small the children know that there must be nothing leavened in the house during Pesaḥ. This is a reminder of the time when their ancestors left in such haste that there was no time for the bread to rise, so they took unleavened bread with them. (⟶ Exodus 12:31–34)

Matzah

*"For the Seder, the special meal we have on the evening of the first day of Pesaḥ, three **matzot** are placed on the table, and a piece of one of them is broken off and hidden somewhere in the room. This is called the **Afikoman**. At the end of the meal the children hunt for it, with the rest of us telling them whether they are 'warm' or 'cold'. Sometimes it's the youngest child who hunts for the Afikoman, but in our family the children hunt for it together. When they find it they are given a small present. In another family we know, the children hide it and their father has to find it."*

"One of my earliest memories of Pesaḥ is matzah and jam. I always looked forward to Pesaḥ, when I could have matzah and jam for breakfast! That was one of my favourite foods. They went together very nicely, matzah and jam. We were always involved in Pesaḥ — obviously not as babies — but as soon as we could eat or walk. We wouldn't stay up for all of it in the early stages. Then when we got older, perhaps seven or eight, we had to prepare a little piece, some anecdote from the Rabbis, which we'd give to everyone , in **shiur** style. We still do that today."

The Seder

Alongside the matzot on the table is the Seder plate. On it are five symbolic foods:

חזרת
Lettuce

זרוע
Roasted Bone

ביצה
Egg

חרוסת
Haroset

מרור
Bitter Herbs

כרפס
Parsley

Seder plate.

— a roasted bone, which represents the Paschal lamb which was sacrificed at the Temple in Jerusalem and eaten during the Passover meal.

— a hard boiled egg, which is a symbol of mourning for the loss of the Temple, destroyed in 70 CE, and of the festival offering made there. (For CE ⟶ page 26.)

— horseradish or other bitter herbs, symbolising the bitter life of the slaves. (⟶ Exodus 1:8−14)

— parsley or some other green vegetable, which is dipped in salt water representing the tears of the slaves in Egypt.

— ḥaroset (a mixture of apple, nut and wine), symbolising the mortar which the slaves made to cement the bricks together.

During the meal, which may last for over four hours, everyone, including the children, drinks four glasses of wine. These are reminders of God's four promises to the Israelites (⟶ Exodus 6:6−7):

'I will bring you out of Egypt.' 'I will deliver you from their bondage.' 'I will redeem you with an outstretched arm.' 'I will take you to me for a people.'

13

*"Because the Seder is so long, sometimes I find some of the parts carry on a bit. We all have our own **Haggadah**. I've got two **Haggadot** — different kinds of translations. My sister asked the questions last year, when she was four. She only did a bit of it — not all four questions. It is in Hebrew, and she needed a bit of help. I did it when I was four or five, when I was the youngest in the family."*

Seder means 'order', and the order for the Pesaḥ meal is set out in a book called a Haggadah, which means 'narrative', 'telling'. Each person has a copy, and the children will probably have a special children's Haggadah, with large print and coloured pictures. Sometimes the pictures have tabs to pull, so in the picture of Moses as a baby in the bulrushes the child can pull the tab and move the baby's ark through the water.

The four questions

An important part of the Seder comes near the beginning of the Haggadah, when the youngest child asks four questions:

'Why is this night different from all other nights? On all other nights we eat either matzah or leavened bread, but on this night matzah only.

On all other nights we eat all kinds of herbs, but on this night we eat bitter herbs.

On all other nights we do not dip herbs even once, but on this night we dip twice.

On all other nights we may eat either sitting or leaning, but on this night we lean.'

The father of the family then tells the story of the Exodus, the escape from slavery. He says, 'Our fathers were in Egypt' or even 'We were in Egypt', so although the Exodus happened more than three thousand years ago, each generation feels very close to that great event. In the story in the Bible, Moses leads the people out of Egypt, but when the father of the family re-tells the story during the Seder, he doesn't mention Moses. He says, 'The Lord brought us out with a strong hand'. Jewish children are therefore reminded at Pesaḥ that it is God who saved his people.

Pesaḥ songs
At the end of the meal, everyone joins in the singing of a number of Pesaḥ songs. The last song to be sung is **Ḥad Gadyah**, 'One Only Kid', and the verses grow just like the verses in *The House that Jack Built*. It is always a great favourite with children. It has come to be interpreted in a special way. The kid stands for the Jewish people, who have suffered at the hands of so many nations, but they are reminded that God, the Holy One, will redeem his people as he did at the Exodus.

One only kid, one only kid,
Which father bought for two zuzim.
    One only kid, one only kid.

And the cat came and ate the kid,
Which father bought for two zuzim.
    One only kid, one only kid.
Then came the dog and bit the cat
That ate the kid,
Which father bought for two zuzim.
    One only kid, one only kid.

And so on, till the last verse is reached:

Then came the Holy One, Blessed be He.
He destroyed the angel of death,
Who slew the slaughterer,
Who killed the ox
That drank up the water
That extinguished the fire
That burnt the stick
That hit the dog that bit the cat
That ate the kid,
Which father bought for two zuzim.
    One only kid, one only kid.

Sukkot

"The festivals are special for children. They bring it all to life. We involve the children in everything. We enjoy seeing them enjoying themselves. It's not just for us, or for the children. It's for us and the children together."

The sukkah

*"We help to decorate the **sukkah**. We make paper chains, and pictures, and hang up oranges and pears and apples and grapes, and other decorations. My brother made a model of a sukkah. Some people in Israel sleep in their sukkah. We didn't manage to eat in the sukkah too much this year, because the weather was terrible."*

A family enjoy a meal under the sukkah.

Jewish people celebrate Sukkot in the autumn. It is a harvest festival, but it is also a reminder of the time when their ancestors

16

were journeying in the wilderness after they had escaped from Egypt. They didn't have solid houses to live in, and they had to build temporary booths, or **sukkot** ($\longrightarrow$ Leviticus 23:42−43). It is the custom now for synagogues to build a very large sukkah for the festival, but observant families like to have their own sukkah at home as well, and to have at least some of their meals out in it. For Sukkot, as for the other festivals in Judaism, there is lots for children to do, helping with the preparations as well as enjoying the celebration itself.

A sukkah has to be out in the open air. It must have at least three walls, so it could be built against the side of a house, and its roof must not be solid − so that the stars can be seen through it. The roof is usually made of branches of greenery. This is a vivid reminder that when the Israelites were living in the wilderness they had only temporary homes.

"When I was only three or four years old we went to stay at a Jewish boarding house run by some people who were friends of my parents and grandparents. They had an enormous sukkah, with beautiful pictures of their ancestors on the wall. It was lovely, and very impressive indeed for a little child. There were loads of people, and quite venerable people − rabbis − but it was very relaxed and friendly."

Lulav

*"You wave the **lulav** in every direction − in front, to your right, backwards over your shoulder, to your left, and then up and down − to show that God is everywhere. Children don't have to wave the lulav, but they enjoy doing it. After Bar Mitzvah you have to do it, so all the adults do. Like lots of other things in Judaism, the children do it if they want to, and it doesn't matter if they don't want to."*

The lulav is made up of four different kinds of plants, called 'the four species' ($\longrightarrow$ Leviticus 23:40). They are small branches of palm and myrtle and willow and an etrog. An etrog is a citrus fruit, rather like a very large lemon, and it is held in the left hand for the ritual of 'waving the lulav'. The three branches, bound together, are held in the right hand, and the hands are held together. The lulav is waved in the synagogue at Sukkot, while the **Hallel** Psalms (113−118) are sung.

Simḥat Torah

*"There's lots of dancing, and lots of fun. They dance between the readings from the **Torah**. Girls do folk dancing. Men dance with the scrolls. I was holding a Torah scroll last year, when I was eight. It was so heavy I couldn't stand up with it."*

"When I was a child we used to have flags for the Simḥat Torah processions, with an apple on top of the stick and candle on top of that. We lit the candle."

*The cover of a scroll is usually silk or velvet. The bells on top and the 'breastplate' hung over it are reminders of the High Priest's garment in biblical times (→ Exodus 28:15–21, 33). A **yad**, which is hung over the scroll, is used to point to the text to avoid touching the scroll.*

Simḥat Torah is one of the few festivals in Judaism which is wholly centred on the synagogue rather than on the home, but it is still very much a celebration for children. They take part in joyful processions when the Torah scrolls are carried round the synagogue. They sing songs and wave flags and banners and small Torah scrolls that they have made. And they have a special part in the service: boys who are under the age of Bar Mitzvah (→ page 59), are called up to the reading of the Torah, and small children may say together one of the prayers which are normally said by adults.

Simḥat Torah means 'Rejoicing of the Torah'. It is a festival that comes just after Sukkot. The first five books of the Jewish Bible are known as the Torah (→ page 36), and the festival celebrates their importance in Judaism. A section of the Torah is read in the synagogue service every Shabbat, and the reading of the whole Torah is completed in a year. On Simḥat Torah the last section of the book of Deuteronomy is read, and this is immediately followed by the reading of the first section of Genesis, the beginning of the next cycle of readings. This is a way of showing, symbolically, that the reading and study of the Torah never cease.

Jewish children learn through this festival how important the Torah is, but the scrolls themselves also show how important it is. Their appearance is very impressive, and they are treated with great respect.

Torah scrolls

The Hebrew for a Torah scroll is ספר תורה – **Sefer Torah.**

The scrolls are made of parchment, and the writing is done by hand. The finished scroll must have no mistakes in it. It can take at least a year for a scribe to complete a Sefer Torah. The scribe must be an expert at writing Hebrew script, but he must also be a very religious person. Torah scrolls are the most holy documents in Judaism. The Hebrew word for a scribe is **sofer**.

When the writing on the scroll is finished, each end of the long roll of parchment is fixed to a wooden roller with handles so that it can be carried without touching the scroll. The two rolls are then held together with a cloth binder.

Sifrei Torah (plural of Sefer Torah) are kept in a special place in the synagogue. It is called the **Aron Ha-kodesh** – the Holy Ark. It is a reminder of the Ark of the Covenant which Moses was told to build for the tablets of the Law – the Ten Commandments – at Mount Sinai. In front of the Aron Ha-kodesh is a curtain, with some of the symbols of Judaism embroidered on it. During a service in the synagogue everybody in the congregation stands when the curtains are drawn back for the Ark to be opened and one of the scrolls to be taken out.

The Sefer Torah is then carried in procession to the **bimah**, a raised platform. In traditional synagogues the bimah is in the middle of the synagogue. Seven passages from the Torah are read during an ordinary Shabbat morning service, and seven men, or boys over the age of thirteen (→ page 59), are called up for the readings. It is an honour for a person to receive an **aliyah** – to be called up. Aliyah is the Hebrew word for 'ascent', 'going up', because the person ascends the bimah for the reading.

Ḥanukkah

*"This never seems as important as other **ḥagim**. It's just a short ceremony in the evening, lighting the candles. But we enjoyed it. We made our own **Ḥanukkiyah**. One I remember was a piece of wood with upturned bottle tops to hold the candles."*

Ḥanukkah is called a minor festival, because it is not a full holiday. There are no regulations about not working as there are with the main festivals. It has become a much more important festival, however, in many families with young children, especially in America. This is because it comes just before the Christian festival of Christmas, and Jewish children could otherwise feel left out of it when the other boys and girls are excitedly looking forward to parties and presents.

*"We heard the story of Judah Maccabee every Ḥanukkah. It's not in the **Tanakh** but we knew it from reading story books. It was really exciting. I used to make a shield for myself and a Judah Maccabee helmet, and prance round the house as Judah Maccabee. When I was seven or eight I had a little tool box of my own and had great fun banging the nails in. I made a shield out of a round piece of wood. I remember clearly putting a big **Magen David** on the shield, and making a sword out of wood. Judah Maccabee was always one of my favourite figures."*

Magen David means 'Shield of David'. It is often called the 'Star of David'. It is a six-pointed star and it is a popular Jewish symbol. It is on the flag of the State of Israel.

Judah Maccabee was a Jewish leader who defeated the Syrian army and regained control of the great Temple in Jerusalem in 165 BCE. (The Greek form of his name is Judas Maccabaeus.) There had been a terrible persecution of the Jews, and those who refused to give up their religion were killed. The Temple had been desecrated by the Syrians, and it had to be cleansed and rededicated before the Jewish people could use it for worship again. Ḥanukkah means 'dedication', and it is the re-dedication of the Temple which the festival celebrates.

One of the candles — the shammash — is used to light the other eight. Each day the new candle is the one which is lit first.

Festival of Lights

Hanukkah is also called the Festival of Lights. There is a tradition that when the Jews regained control of the Temple, they found only one container of the sacred oil that was used for the **Ner Tamid** — the Everlasting Light — which burned day and night in the Temple. There was only enough oil to keep the lamp burning for one day, but miraculously it lasted for eight days until the High Priest could consecrate more oil. This is why Hanukkah lasts for eight days.

*"At Hanukkah we play a game with a **dreidl** and counters. We mostly use nuts as counters, though sometimes we play with pennies. The dreidl has a Hebrew letter on each of its sides. You take turns to spin it."*

> The Hebrew letters on a dreidl are the first letters of the words שָׁם הָיָה גָּדֹל נֵס — nes = miracle, gadol = great, hayah = happened, and sham = there.

> The story of the Maccabaean Revolt against the Syrians is told in I Maccabees, one of the books in the Apocrypha, attached to the Christian Bible. You can read about the persecution of the Jews in the first chapter.

Children celebrating Purim.

Purim

*"In the synagogue, there's a reading of the **Megillah**. The children have football rattles and some of them have cap guns. One of the things our children make at Hebrew class is yoghurt cartons filled with dried beans. There's a sort of game where the reader tries to sneak in a 'Haman' without anyone hearing it, but I've never known any reader to win that game. In Israel it's more like a carnival, with the whole country involved. It's more of a national festival, because it's about freedom from the oppressor."*

Megillah is a small parchment scroll that is fixed to a roller only at one end. The word usually refers to the book of Esther in the Bible.

Purim is an exciting time for Jewish children. They make masks or paint their faces, and dress up as one of the characters in the story in the book of Esther. They have fancy dress parties, but they also wear their costumes to the synagogue for the reading of the Megillah. The story tells how more than two thousand years ago Esther saved her people when the wicked court official, Haman, planned to kill all the Jews in the Persian empire. The children listen intently as the story is read, because the idea is not to let the name of Haman be heard. They soon get to know the story when they are little; they have to know when Haman is going to be mentioned, and they drown out his name with shouts and football rattles and anything that makes a loud noise!

Read the story of Esther in the Bible. How many times does the name of Haman have to be drowned out?

Rosh Ha-Shanah

"It's a tradition to have apples and honey at Rosh Ha-Shanah. Dad cuts an apple in pieces, puts some honey on them and passes one to each of us. It represents the sweetness we hope for in the new year. Some people have raisins in their ḥallah. We put honey on the ḥallah — on Shabbats and other festival days — from Rosh Ha-Shanah right through to Simḥat Torah, because our family likes honey!"

'Le-shanah tovah!' That is how Jews greet each other at New Year. It means 'For a good year', which is a shortened form of the wish 'May God write you down for a good year in the Book of Life'. This wish is used on the greetings cards which people send to friends and relatives at Rosh Ha-Shanah.

> In Hebrew, **rosh** means 'head' and **shanah** means 'year', so this festival is the 'head of the year', the beginning of the new year.

A New Year card.

Many people have different shaped ḥallah at Rosh Ha-Shanah. Instead of the long plaited ḥallot, they make it round, symbolising the way the year goes round — ending and beginning again. Sometimes a crown is put round the ḥallah, symbolising God as king.

Rosh Ha-Shanah is a joyous festival, but it is also the beginning of a ten day period in which Jewish people are encouraged to examine the kind of life they have lived through the past year. For children, it is the celebration, with its songs and special foods and new clothes, which is most important, but they will hear the **shofar** blown in the synagogue, they will hear the story of the binding of Isaac read, and they will know that the adults are looking back over the year and trying to put right whatever has gone wrong in their lives.

Shofar

The shofar is a curved ram's horn. In biblical times it was blown at the beginning of each month and on a number of other special occasions, but now it is blown only in the month of Elul (the month leading up to Rosh Ha-Shanah), at Rosh Ha-Shanah itself and at the end of Yom Kippur (⟶ page 25). The ram's horn is a reminder of the story of the ram which was caught by its horns in a thicket, and which Abraham sacrificed instead of his son Isaac (⟶ Genesis 22).

"The shofar makes a marvellous sound, especially for the **tekiah gedolah** *— the long wailing note which is blown at the end of Yom Kippur and three times on Rosh Ha-Shanah. It's very difficult to blow the shofar. Dad has one, and it's only since I was about sixteen that I've managed to get a reasonable sound from it. You need an awful lot of breath."*

The Shofar is a curved ram's horn, a reminder of the story in Genesis 22.

Design a Rosh Ha-Shanah card with appropriate Jewish symbols.

Yom Kippur

"I was always impressed by the solemnity at Yom Kippur. It's quite a long time. As a child you notice that, and everyone around you is solemn, praying."

"I take the children to the synagogue for as long as they can keep quiet. The two year old was in one of her moods this year so it didn't turn out to be very long!"

Yom Kippur (the Day of Atonement) comes at the end of the ten days which begin with Rosh Ha-Shanah. It is the most solemn day in the Jewish calendar. Observant Jews will fast for the twenty-five hours from sunset on the eve of Yom Kippur till nightfall the next day, and they may spend all that time in the synagogue. Even those Jews who don't bother much about religious observance will try to spend at least some time in the synagogue at Yom Kippur.

Yom Kippur is a time for confessing one's sins and asking God's forgiveness. But it is also a time for asking forgiveness from people whom one has hurt or wronged, because Jews believe that they cannot be forgiven unless they are genuinely determined to put right what has gone wrong.

"This year I fasted till lunch time. Next year I'm going to try to fast all day. My sister fasted last year when she was eleven. She likes books and I don't, so she reads and she forgets about it, or she talks with her friends. Children stay in the house mainly, not eating any sweets. We have a competition to see who can last the longest."

"We used to fast as long back as I can remember. We'd at least make some effort, like not having breakfast so early, or waiting till lunch. In the afternoons, when we broke our fast, my sister and I, we'd have some food in a bag and we'd go outside the synagogue. You go outside every hour or so for a breath of fresh air. When I was a bit older I'd go outside to take my turn guarding the doors. Shul has had some bomb alerts in the past. We have to have a couple of people on the doors if we want to have them open. That's for all the festivals, but particularly Yom Kippur and Rosh Ha-Shanah, when people know that there are crowds in the synagogue."

The calendar

Jewish children have two different calendars. For them 1 January 2000 will also be 23 Tevet 5760.

The Jewish calendar begins 3,761 years before the Christian calendar. This date was chosen many centuries ago, because it was believed that that was when the world was created. So the letters AM are put after the year – 5760 AM. AM are the initial letters of the Latin words Anno Mundi, meaning 'in the year of the world' – 'the year since creation'.

The international calendar uses BC, 'Before Christ' (that is, before the Messiah) and AD, Anno Domini 'in the year of the Lord'. This way of counting years uses Christian beliefs about the person of Jesus which are not shared by non-Christians. So the practice of using BCE and CE was introduced for speaking and writing about Judaism. These letters stood for 'Before the Common Era' and 'in the Common Era'. Gradually BCE and CE came to be used in the study of all religions. However, the other world religions don't share a 'common era' with Christianity in the way that Judaism does, so many people now think of the letters standing for 'Before the Christian Era' and 'in the Christian Era'.

Lunar year

The Jewish year is lunar (calculated by the moon) so it has twelve months of 29½ days, shorter than a solar year. If no adjustment was made, the festivals would occur eleven days earlier each year, and the spring festival of Pesaḥ would move back into the winter and then into the autumn!

The problem is solved by having leap years, with thirteen months, in every cycle of nineteen years – the 3rd, 6th, 8th, 11th, 14th, 17th and 19th years. In leap years the month Adar is called Adar I and the extra month is called Adar II.

It takes the moon 29½ days to complete its cycle, waxing from new moon to full moon, and then waning until the next new moon appears. To avoid having months of 29½ days each, the first month in the year has 30 days, the next has 29, and so on. In leap years, Adar I has 30 days and Adar II has 29.

The months

Nisan	(March/April)	Tishri	(September/October)
Iyyar	(April/May)	Ḥeshvan	(October/November)
Sivan	(May/June)	Kislev	(November/December)
Tammuz	(June/July)	Tevet	(December/January)
Av	(July/August)	Shevat	(January/February)
Elul	(August/September)	Adar	(February/March)

Major festivals

Pesaḥ (Passover): 15−22 Nisan
Shavuot (Pentecost): 6−7 Sivan
Sukkot (Tabernacles):15−23 Tishri
   Simḥat Torah (Rejoicing of the Torah): 23 Tishri

Minor and modern festivals

Ḥanukkah (Lights): 25 Kislev−2 Tevet
Purim (Lots): 14 Adar
Yom Ha'atzmaut (Israel Independence Day): 5 Iyyar
Tu B'Shevat (New Year for Trees): 15 Shevat

High Holy Days

Rosh Ha-Shanah (New Year): 1−2 Tishri
Yom Kippur (Day of Atonement): 10 Tishri

Fasts

Tisha B'Av (Mourning for the loss of the Temple): 9 Av
Yom Ha-Shoah (Holocaust Day): 27 Nisan

For Orthodox Jews, the festivals (except for Rosh Ha-Shanah) last one day longer in the Diaspora − countries outside Israel − than they do in Israel. This custom goes a long way back in history. Before there was a fixed calendar, a month began when the new moon was seen in Jerusalem. This could be on either the 29th or the 30th day. Jewish communities a long way from Jerusalem would not hear in time for the beginning of festivals so, to make sure, they celebrated them on two days.

Can you think of some imaginative ways of showing the Jewish calendar and the festivals?

Yom Ha'atzmaut

Through most of their festivals Jewish children learn about the experiences of their people many centuries ago, but Judaism also has modern festivals as well. Yom Ha'atzmaut — Israel Independence Day — celebrates the creation of the State of Israel in 1948.

"In Cambridge Yom Ha'atzmaut is nothing really. I celebrated it once in Israel, and it's amazing, it's incredible. At night, on the eve of the festival everybody goes out on the streets. You have little plastic hammers with sponge things at one end. When you hit with them they make a noise, so you hit people on the head with them. People running round, hitting people on the head! There are fireworks, and all kinds of singers along the road. It's such a feeling of aliveness."

"Israel is always what I have felt most strongly about, in all of being Jewish. This passion for a homeland. The Jews never had it, and now we do have it. I want to go and live in Israel. I want to give my children what I never had, that they should be born in Israel, and be Israeli."

Tu B'Shevat

"Tu B'Shevat is not such a big festival. You just plant a tree, but not last year, when we were in Israel, because it was the 7th year. The trees are planted in the Forest of Jerusalem, where there are lots of hills and the ground is all flaky, and it needs support. And there are some other places in the north. People who don't live there can give money for trees. In this country we pay 20p to get a sticker. There are ten stickers in a row, and every row is a tree."

> The seventh year is called a sabbatical year, from the word 'sabbath'. In biblical times the land was allowed to rest for a year every seven years (⟶ Leviticus 25:1−7)

Yom Ha-Shoah

Yom Ha-Shoah (Holocaust Day) is a fast rather than a festival. It is a time of mourning for the six million Jews who were killed in' Europe during the Holocaust, when the Nazis tried to wipe out Judaism. In Jerusalem wreaths are laid at Yad Vashem, which was built as a memorial to those who died in the Holocaust. The story is told, in words and pictures, of the events which led up to the Holocaust and the tragic suffering of those who were sent to concentration camps.

"We went to Yad Vashem when I was in Israel. I went twice, once with my school. It was almost too much. At the beginning it's interesting, but when it gets to the 'final solution' . . . Six million Jews died. I'm glad I wasn't alive then. Our grandpa and his parents were there. They died in the war. Their brothers and sisters died in the concentration camps."

"I went to Yad Vashem when I was seven, and on all my visits since. I carry that with me all the time. Even in my happiest moments, anything can make you just think back; it makes you stop and think for a minute. I'm not highly strung, I don't burst into tears. I just have it with me all the time. What I've always found most satisfying at Yad Vashem is seeing the avenue for non-Jewish people who gave help. There's a tree planted for everybody who gave help, and for a Jew that is most moving and rewarding, because the feeling of isolation is so great at times."

A flame burns continually in the hall at Yad Vashem where the names of all the concentration camps are carved in the stone floor.

"There is a special new memorial in Yad Vashem. You go through a door into a passage which leads right round a large room. The room is pitch-black except for the effect of thousands and thousands of flickering flames — one for each child who died in the Holocaust. There is only one candle in the room, but it is reflected in thousands of tiny mirrors all over the room. A voice recites the names and ages of the children killed — names and more names. For me it is one of the most emotional places in Israel."

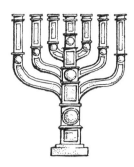

A way of life

Learning by doing

"Small children like imitating adults, and there are many things for children to do, on a day-to-day basis. For example, any time you're having a meal where you are having a blessing over the bread, you wash your hands, and the children do it too — from when they are little. We wouldn't make an issue of it if they wanted to run off, but they tend to like doing it. We touch the **mezuzah** *by the front door when we come into the house and even when the children were no more than babies they wanted to be lifted up to touch it too."*

There are many symbolic actions in Judaism, and this is one of the ways in which children come to learn about their religion. The symbols are reminders of what is important in the religion. A mezuzah is a reminder that this is a Jewish home, and that the family who live there observe God's Torah.

Torah is a difficult Hebrew word to translate into English. Perhaps the best word is 'teaching'. It is often translated as 'law', but that can give quite the wrong impression. The **mitzvot**, or commandments, of Judaism are not at all like the laws of a country. If people break any of the country's laws they can be prosecuted, but each Jewish person decides how far he or she will observe the mitzvot. This is why a person who chooses to keep the mitzvot in a very disciplined way is described as 'observant'. Jews who belong to the Orthodox section of Judaism are the most observant. There are other movements within Judaism, such as Reform, Conservative, Progressive and Hassidic, which interpret Torah in different ways. This book is mainly about the way of life of observant Jews.

Mezuzah

The Hebrew word mezuzah means doorpost, and in an observant home a mezuzah will be fixed to the right hand side of the front door and of all the other doors in the house except those which lead into a room that is used for purely personal toilet purposes, such as bathrooms and toilets.

A mezuzah is a small case, usually made of metal or wood, with a rolled up piece of parchment inside it. On it, written by hand, are two passages from the Bible: Deuteronomy 6:4−9 and 11:13−21. These passages are part of the **Shema** (⟶ page 40). On the outside of the case is the Hebrew letter ‏שׁ‎ (shin), or perhaps the word ‏שַׁדַּי‎ (**Shaddai**), which means Almighty and is one of the names of God.

Make an imitation mezuzah or draw a picture of one. Copy out the biblical passages which go in the mezuzah.

Kippah

Another symbol is the **kippah**, or skullcap, which many Jewish men and boys wear while they are praying. Some observant Jews wear a kippah all the time. Another name for a kippah is **yarmulka.** This is a Yiddish word.

Yiddish is a language which was developed by Jews who lived in Eastern Europe in the medieval period. It is based on two languages − German and Hebrew.

"How people react to me depends on whether I'm wearing my kippah. If I'm not I don't actually appear Jewish. There's a lot of anti-semitism. I often met it when I was walking to the youth group at the synagogue with my sister on a Saturday afternoon. Boys used to shout at us, and throw pennies at us − this idea of Jews being mean! I used to regret that it was Shabbat, when you don't carry things. Otherwise I'd have picked them up. I'd have made quite a collection!"

Tallit

A tallit is worn during morning prayers, both at home and in the synagogue. Small children are therefore very familiar with it, and come to learn its significance. The important part of it is the fringes which hang from its four corners. There is a mitzvah in the Bible (Numbers 15:37−41) which commands males to put fringes on the corners of their garments, so that when they see them they are reminded of God's commandments.

A tallit is like a large rectangular scarf. It is white, and it has blue or black stripes at each end. The fringes are made by putting four threads through a hole at each corner, folding them over (to make eight threads), and tieing them together with five knots.

Kashrut

"When you go to a party you have to remember what you can eat and what you can't eat. At school, when they don't know that you keep **kosher** *they offer you all kinds of food — flavoured crisps, chewing gum — and you have to say, sorry, you can't eat it. We can't eat sweets that have got gelatine in, and that kind of thing. And E numbers are also difficult because they sometimes have animal fat in. My friend always makes me pizza. She tells me that I shouldn't think that she lives on pizza; it's just that she doesn't know what else to give me!"*

"In my school in London, when I say that I can't eat something, some people make racist remarks. But this year, in religious education we have been learning something about each religion, and since we started those classes a lot of people have come up and said that they were really sorry for what they had said."

The word kosher means 'proper' or 'fit to eat', and **kashrut** is the name given to the laws which govern kosher food. The basic laws are set out in the Torah (Leviticus 11), but here is an outline of what they involve.

Kosher foods are:
1 Meat from animals which both chew the cud and have cloven hooves (e.g. sheep, cows and goats, but not pigs).
2 Fish which have both fins and scales (e.g. cod and herrings, but not eels or shell fish).
3 Birds which are domesticated (e.g. chickens, geese and turkeys, but not birds of prey).
4 Eggs and milk from kosher birds and animals.

Food which is forbidden is called **tref** and food which is neither milk nor meat (e.g. fruit and vegetables) is called **pareve.**

"Children learn gradually what is kosher and what is not. For example, when we were all out together shopping, and one of them would ask me why we couldn't buy those biscuits over there, I would say 'They aren't kosher; we'll buy kosher biscuits,' or 'I'll make them

at home'. If they wanted an iced lollie, or something, I'd say, 'Let's look at the ingredients and see if they are kosher'. If you experience that when you are little, then by the time you get to eight or nine you do it for yourself."

In towns and cities with a large Jewish community there are kosher butchers and shops selling kosher cakes and other foods.

Milk and meat

Kashrut also involves not eating meat and milk at the same meal. Observant families keep two sets of cutlery and crockery, one for meat dishes and one for milk dishes, so the children soon learn that meat and milk have to be kept separate. They also learn how long they must wait after a meat meal before having anything with milk or other dairy products in it, and vice versa.

"We don't have milk for at least three hours after a meat meal, and meat for at least half an hour after a meal with milk in it, but we have friends who leave six hours after a meat meal and one hour after a milk meal."

> Plan the menu for a two or three course meal for entertaining a Jewish friend who keeps kosher. Don't forget about separate meat and milk dishes.

Learning Hebrew

"The service in the synagogue is all in Hebrew. I can follow it but I can't understand it without the English, so I go to Hebrew classes."

Hebrew is a very ancient language. It has continued to be used for worship and study, but it stopped being a language for everyday use until about a century ago.

Earlier in this book you met the Hebrew alphabet. In ancient times Hebrew was written without the vowels. This is called 'unpointed' Hebrew, and it is how the Hebrew Bible was written. But it is not only biblical Hebrew that is unpointed. In Israel you can find newspapers, public notices, signposts, advertisements and so on without any vowels in the writing.

> If you saw buses with these names on the front, where would they be going? בֵּית־לֶחֶם נָצְרַת

Hebrew vowels

The system of dots and dashes for writing vowels is rather complicated, but here are some guidelines which you can refer to as you meet Hebrew words. Don't try to learn all this at once! These are just notes for reference if you like working out puzzles.

> 1 Words always begin with a consonant, so one couldn't have a word like the English word 'above'. The word אָדָם (Adam) doesn't begin with the vowel 'a' but with the consonant Alef, which has no sound, like the letter 'h' in the English word 'hour'.
>
> 2 Most of the signs which represent vowels go under the consonant which they follow. For example, in the word for 'year' – שָׁנָה (shanah) – the first 'a' goes under the שׁ (sh) and the second 'a' goes under the נ (n).
>
> 3 There are two vowel signs that don't go under letters. The sign for 'o' goes above the consonant: סֹפֵר and the one for long 'u' is put half way up the consonant: לוּלָב Did you recognise sofer and lulav?

Here are some of the main vowel signs. (In modern Israeli Hebrew the long vowels are pronounced just like the short vowels.)

ָ	Long a, as in sh<u>a</u>nah	שָׁנָה	} pronounced as in *bat*
ַ	Short a, as in h<u>a</u>llah	חַלָּה	
ֵ or יֵ	Long e, as in s<u>e</u>fer	סֵפֶר	} pronounced as in *bet*
ֶ	Short e, as in p<u>e</u>sah	פֶּסַח	
ִ or יִ	Long i, as in nevi'<u>i</u>m	נְבִיאִים	} pronounced as in *bit*
ִ	Short i, as in m<u>i</u>tzvah	מִצְוָה	
ֹ or וֹ	Long o, as in t<u>o</u>rah	תּוֹרָה	pronounced as in *top*
ֻ	Long u, as in kashr<u>u</u>t	כַּשְׁרוּת	} pronounced as in *put*
ֻ	Short u, as in s<u>u</u>kkot	סֻכּוֹת	

The long vowels which are written like this: יֵ (e), יִ (i), וֹ (o), וּ (u), are the ones which were represented by consonants before the system of pointing Hebrew was invented.

Here are some more guidelines which you might find useful.

1 There are two main ways to form a plural noun. One way is to add 'im' יִם at the end: חַג hag, חַגִּים hagim; but if the noun ends in 'ah' הָ the 'ah' is changed to 'ot' וֹת : סֻכָּה sukkah, סֻכּוֹת sukkot.

2 The word for 'the' (ha) is always joined to its noun. So 'the year' is hashanah' – הַשָּׁנָה

3 In English the adjective comes before the noun it is describing: 'loud music', but in Hebrew the adjective comes after the noun. You say 'yom tov' – 'good day'.

4 A dot in the middle of a consonant (except at the beginning of a word) is not a vowel sign; it often shows that the consonant is doubled: שַׁבָּת Shabbat.

What names do these Jewish children have? רָחֵל דָּוִד שָׂרָה

Learning from the past

There are so many things to do in Judaism, and when children are little they learn what to do by watching other people and joining in. But Jewish people have always valued study, and observant families put a lot of emphasis on the Jewish education of their children.

"We had a large illustrated book of Bible stories for children — the Rupert Bear type of book, with line drawings and speech in balloons coming from the characters' mouths. It was done by a Jewish firm. It was brilliant. It would bring it all to life. Mum and Dad used to read it to us in the early stages, and then we used to read it for ourselves, and later we would recognise the stories in the Haftarot, which was fun."

> **Haftarot** are the biblical passages which are read in the synagogue service after the passages from the Torah have been read. They come from the section of the Bible called the Prophets.

The Torah

However, the Bible is more than stories. The most important part of the Bible for observant Jews is the Torah, the five Books of Moses which come at the beginning of the Bible. It is the foundation on which Judaism is built.

> The Jewish Bible is often called the Tanakh. This is not a real Hebrew word; it is made up of the first letters of Torah, **Nevi'im** (Prophets), and **Ketuvim** (Writings) — the three sections of the Bible.
>
> The Hebrew Bible was also the Bible of the first Christians, though the Christians later called it the Old Testament, and followed a different order for the books. The order of the Hebrew Bible is:
>
> Torah: the first five books — Genesis to Deuteronomy;
> Nevi'im: the Former Prophets (Joshua, Judges, Samuel, Kings) and the Latter Prophets (Isaiah, Jeremiah, Ezekiel) and the twelve 'minor' or short books (Hosea to Malachi);
> Ketuvim (Writings): All the rest of the books.

Make a list of the books in the Hebrew Bible under the headings of the three sections, and check how different it is from the order of the books in the Christian Old Testament.

An illuminated manuscript from a book about the Law by the twelfth century Jewish scholar Maimonides.

Knowing why

"There's a lot of misunderstanding about Judaism. Our nine year old is the only Jewish boy in his school. The only way you can prepare him is to make him secure in what he knows. It's not just something he does but something he knows about. If we just said, 'You do this', and didn't explain why, he wouldn't feel so secure."

"Dad teaches me most mornings before I go to school. We get about 15 minutes. We do translating — of the Tanakh — and we've been doing Jewish history. We started with King David, and now we're in the seventeenth century, so we've come a long way."

Children in observant families learn Hebrew, because the Tanakh is in Hebrew and so are the services in the synagogue. But there are also lots of other things to learn. They learn about the mitzvot in the Torah, like the mitzvah about parents teaching their children (⟶ Deuteronomy 6:7).

"I started learning the Torah when I was about eight. I'm now going through Samuel and Deuteronomy."

This girl is learning at home with her father, but she is also studying in a Hebrew class at the synagogue.

"There is no reason for girls not to have the same Jewish education as the boys. My grandfather was a rabbi, and in the school holidays he used to come round every morning and give my two brothers and me Hebrew lessons. We were all learning at the same level."

Talmud

"With Dad I learn **Mishnah**. *Dad's got all the volumes of the Talmud. It's really giant! I've learnt* **Berakhot**. *I'm also looking at the* **Gemara**. *It's harder. It's just a continuation of the Mishnah."*

This eleven year old girl has begun the kind of study which Orthodox Jews continue throughout their whole life.

"Dad regularly gives a shiur, where people come to the house to learn Talmud, so it was just natural for me to learn with him. From the age of twelve I used to get up at 6 o'clock — I still do — and get dressed, and Dad and I pray together, and then we have half an hour shiur on a particular piece of Talmud. For me at the beginning it wasn't the Talmud itself that mattered; it was setting aside an hour in the day when I was with Dad. We were together and we were learning something Jewish."

> The word 'talmud' means 'study'. The Talmud is not a book; it is a whole library of books. It contains stories, parables, teachings and discussions about everything that is important in putting Judaism into practice.

Jews believe that God has shown them in the Torah how he wants them to live. However, the conditions in which people live gradually change, so they had to ask, 'How do we apply the mitzvot in the Torah in today's world?' And Orthodox Jews have gone on asking that question ever since.

The discussion about how to apply the mitzvot that were in the Torah — the Written Law — began way back in biblical times, and the teachings that grew out of the discussion are called the Oral Law, or the Oral Tradition. The Oral Tradition grew so much that in about 200 CE a famous scholar called Judah Ha-Nasi (Judah the Prince) made a systematic collection of it. This is known as the Mishnah.

> If you transliterate the Hebrew word at the left hand side of the top line of the page of the Talmud (opposite), you will find out which section it comes from.

Mishnah

The Mishnah is divided into six sections, and in each section there are a number of topics, rather like chapters. The first section of the Mishnah is called 'Seeds' because it deals with all sorts of things to do with the produce of the land — like the offering of the first-fruits at harvest times, and leaving the land to rest every seventh year. The first topic in this section is called Berakhot, which is the Hebrew word for blessings. It includes discussion among the Rabbis about the blessings, like Kiddush and Ha-Motzi (⟶ page 5), which are to be said over different kinds of foods.

Knowing about the laws

"When I was young I can't remember what I thought about the Talmud, apart from being pleased that I was doing it. But now I find it really interesting. It's not only knowing the laws. It's learning how the laws came about, all the arguments they had, and all the discussions. It really sharpens the mind, especially in the mornings before breakfast!"

In the centre of each page of an edition of the Talmud is quite a short passage from the Mishnah and a longer passage from the Gemara. Gemara means 'completion', and the Mishnah and the Gemara together make up the Talmud. Around the text of the Talmud are placed commentaries and discussions about the teaching in that piece of text. These were written later by famous Jewish scholars.

The Tanakh and the Talmud are the foundation on which all later Jewish study has been built.

A page of the Talmud looks complicated, but it is actually arranged to make study easier. It is like having several books that you want to use all open at the right page!

Worship

"We were not taught to say prayers when we were very little, but when we went to bed at night — my sister and I were in bunk beds — Dad would come and sit with us and sing the Shema. It's from the Torah, so it has its special notes for singing. We gradually picked it up and we would join in. That's how we learned it."

Children hear the Shema so often — in the synagogue and at home — that they are made aware of how important it is. It is one of the passages from the Torah which are placed in a mezuzah, and it is also one of the passages in **tefillin** (⟶ page 60).

The Shema has been called Judaism's creed. It is a statement of faith rather than a prayer addressed to God. It begins:

'Hear, O Israel, the Lord is our God, the Lord is One.'
Sh'ma' Yisra'el Adonai Elohenu Adonai 'eḥad.

The Shema gets its name from its first word. 'Shema' is Hebrew for 'hear'. The first word of a prayer or a passage from the Bible is often used as its name.

The Shema consists of three passages from the Torah: Deuteronomy 6:4–9 and 11:13–21 and Numbers 15:37–41.

Prayers

Just as in so many other things in Judaism, it is adults who are expected to pray, rather than children. In observant families younger children see their father and older brothers davening.

*"When the children were little my husband prayed at home in the morning. He used a **Siddur** which was the same size and shape as two small dictionaries we had, and the children were too young to be able to read but they took these dictionaries and pretended they were praying with him. They would argue about whether they wanted the blue one or the black one!"*

These boys, in a children's synagogue, are following the service in the Siddur. Notice the Ten Commandments above the Aron Ha-Kodesh.

At the back of the Siddur there are some morning and evening prayers for children, but whether any of these are used will depend on the family. In some families the children will learn one or more of these prayers when they are about eight or nine years old. One of the prayers is the first verse of the Shema. Here is one of the others:

'Blessed be the Lord by day; blessed be the Lord by night. Blessed be the Lord when we lie down; blessed be the Lord when we rise up.'

This is how many Jewish prayers begin:

בָּרוּךְ אַתָּה יהוה אֱלֹהֵינוּ מֶלֶךְ הָעוֹלָם

barukh attah adonai elohenu melek ha-'olam
'Blessed are you, O Lord our God, King of the universe.'

Amidah

"The Shema is usually the first thing that children learn. But it's not till later that you learn the actual details of the other prayers, what you say in the **Amidah**.*"*

> The word amidah means 'standing', and the prayer is given this name because people always stand while it is being said. The Amidah is one of the most important prayers in Judaism. It is also one of the oldest. It was written about two thousand years ago. It consists of nineteen sets of blessings or berakhot. The oldest ones are the first three, which praise God, and the last three, which are thanksgivings. In between are thirteen petitions, asking God for such things as understanding, forgiveness, healing and the coming of the Messiah. On Shabbats and other festivals the petitions are left out; on these joyful occasions the emphasis is put on praising and thanking God.

Blessings

Much of the worship in the Siddur is in the form of blessings, but there are also blessings for all sorts of things that happen during the day.

"When the children were tiny and were being given an apple or some other fruit, we would say the blessing for eating fruit: 'Blessed are you, O Lord our God, King of the universe, who makes the fruit of the tree.' It would be easy for them to learn it that way. And if there was thunder, we would say the blessing for hearing thunder: 'Blessed are you, O Lord our God, King of the universe, whose strength and might fill the world.'"

> Here are some of the other berakhot:
>
> On seeing a rainbow: 'Blessed are you, O Lord our God, King of the universe, who remembers his covenant and is faithful to his covenant and keeps his promise.'
>
> On hearing good news: 'Blessed are you, O Lord our God, King of the universe, who is good and does good.'
>
> On hearing bad news: 'Blessed are you, O Lord our God, King of the universe, the true Judge.'

Observant families always say grace before and after meals. There are different blessings depending on the kind of food that is being eaten, but here is one that may be said after the meal:

'Blessed are you, O Lord our God, King of the universe, who creates innumerable living beings and their needs, for all the things you have created to sustain every living being. Blessed are you who are the life of the universe.'

Synagogue service

"One of my earliest memories of Shabbat is sitting with my Dad in shul plaiting his tallit."

Children go to synagogue with their parents on Shabbat morning, and they gradually learn to follow the prayers and readings in the Siddur.

"When I was about nine or ten I was taught how to sing one of the songs that is sung at the end of the service on Saturday morning. It's traditional in many synagogues for a child to lead that song. Ours was a small community so I had that honour to myself until my younger brother learned how to do it."

In an Orthodox synagogue the bimah is in the centre. In a Reform synagogue it is just in front of the Aron Ha-Kodesh.

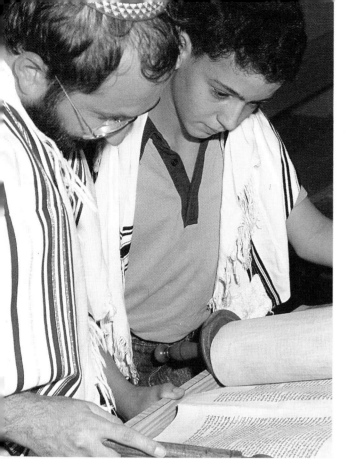

Belief

"For the children, God is just there. Your faith is based so much on the scriptures that you get some idea of God from the Bible. But one can't define God, so one can't really say that he is like this or like that. The basic principle of Judaism is that God gave the Law to Moses — the Written Law and the Oral Law — and they are passed on from one generation to the next. If you ask what makes you Jewish, it's not necessarily a belief in God that is the first thing that comes to mind. You would say that you observe Shabbat, or you observe kashrut. It's what you observe rather than what you believe."

The Torah shows Jews how God wants them to live.

Doing God's will

Observant Jews believe that it is much more important to do what God wants than to discuss what God is like. This doesn't mean that God is unimportant to them. In fact, it's just the opposite. Their whole life is dedicated to trying to live according to God's will, his Torah. The Hebrew word for the laws they observe is **Halakhah**. It means 'walking'. There are many passages in the Bible which describe doing God's will as 'walking'. One of them is the first verse of Psalm 119:

'Blessed are those whose way is blameless,
    who walk in the law of the Lord.'

Psalm 119 is written in a most unusual way. It has 176 verses which are divided into 22 sections. The eight verses in each section start with the same letter of the Hebrew alphabet. Verses 1—8 begin with Alef, verses 9—16 with Bet, and so on. Some English Bibles print the Hebrew letters at the beginning of each section.

> Read Psalm 119: 14–16 and 129–130 and write out one or more of the verses that show what God's Law means to an observant Jew.

Although Orthodox Jews feel that it is more important to be getting on with observing God's Torah than discussing beliefs about him, they do, of course, have beliefs. The main one is expressed in the Shema (—→ page 40).

> Read the Shema again, and using this and other prayers and observances you have learnt about, make a list of the beliefs which are expressed in them.

Names for God

There are many names for God in Judaism – Almighty, King of the Universe, Lord, the Eternal Living One and the Holy One. Many people call God Ha-Shem, which just means 'The Name'.

Jews never refer to God by the personal name which was used in ancient times. They feel that it would not be showing respect to God. This is how it was written – יהוה – but no one now is certain how it was pronounced. When people came across the consonants for God's name in the Bible they said **Adonai**, which means 'Lord'.

> Write down as many examples as you can find, from this book and other sources, of how Jewish people show respect to God.

The future

"When I was young I don't remember anyone talking about the Messiah very much. The belief that Messiah will come is just there."

"There's a concept of the afterlife but it's not stressed. Our daughter was eight when my father died, and she told my mother, who lived in London, that in the world to come she could go to Israel and go shopping with my father in Tel Aviv, because she knew that my mother liked to go shopping!"

Just as Jews don't feel that it is important to speculate about God, so they don't feel that it is important to speculate about the future. What matters is how one lives in this life. The future can safely be left to God.

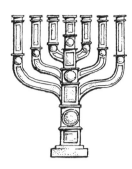

Belonging

Family

"On Shabbat we have a chance to play games with the whole family together."

Shabbat is one of the ways in which Jewish people express the close relationship there is within families. No one will be going shopping, or taking the car to the garage, or going to a meeting. Everyone can relax, and there is plenty of time to do things together – to play games or go for walks or visit friends or relatives. And the children know that they will be able to talk to their parents, and their parents will have time to listen to them.

Parents and children

"Being blessed by Dad has come to mean a lot to me. It's one of the things that make you homesick, the things that you miss, when you are away. Now when we are away, Dad blesses us when he comes to see us. My sister has left school and she is in Israel for a year, and every Friday evening when they've sung Shalom Aleiḥem, she thinks, 'What are they doing at home?' I'm getting blessed and she's not getting blessed by anybody. So Dad blesses her when he goes there, not just because he wants to, but because she wants it."

"When my cousin was married, her father didn't make a speech at the reception. Instead he blessed her and the bridegroom. That was marvellous. I'd like my father to do that for me when I get married."

When a Jewish father blesses his children on Friday evening, it is not just because he is expected to do it as part of the Shabbat ritual (⟶ page 7). It is a way of expressing the very strong bond that exists between parents and children. So it is quite natural for him to bless them on other occasions as well. And because grown-ups are still their parents' children, some Jewish fathers bless their sons and daughters even when they are grown-up.

Women and girls

"The most influential person in the home is the woman. Her role is keeping a kosher home and educating the children while they are young. She might have a job, and go out to work, but keeping a

46

kosher home and making sure that there is food for Shabbat tend to be her responsibility. Her husband will help to a smaller or greater degree, depending on the relationship, just as in non-Jewish homes."

The respect in which the woman of the house is held is expressed in one of the Shabbat evening customs. Her husband, and the rest of the family, sing Eshet Hayil, which begins, 'A woman of worth who can find? Her price is far above rubies. The heart of her husband trusts in her.' This is a poem from Proverbs, a book in the Writings section of the Tanakh (Proverbs 31:10−31).

"Girls and boys know what they can do and what they can't do. The girl knows that she doesn't have to put tefillin on; and I know the berakhot that she makes when she lights the Shabbat candles, though I won't have to light the candles − unless I'm on my own."

One of the reasons for the different responsibilities which men and women have in Judaism is that some of these responsibilities are 'time-bound'. For example, prayers have to be said at certain times. Women would not be expected to stop looking after their children, especially if the children were sick, to go and say the prayers. Of course, Orthodox Jewish women pray, but they don't have to say the regular morning, afternoon and evening prayers.

Judaism is a religion which is based in the home and family. So for observant Jews, the role of the woman is very important. It has been said that Judaism could survive without the synagogue, but it could not survive without the home. Another of the responsibilities of the woman of the house is the kindling of the Shabbat lights. She marks the beginning of Shabbat by performing that ritual.

Marriage

"When I get married it will be to someone who is Orthodox. It matters a lot who you marry. It wouldn't be possible to observe the mitzvot if your wife wasn't observant too."

"It's important to us that our children should not marry out of the faith. But obviously we have to leave the choice to them. All we can do is bring them up with knowledge and awareness of who they are and what they want. I stayed within Judaism probably because of my strong religious background."

Marriage is one of the mitzvot in the Torah. For the ceremony the bride and bridegroom stand under a **ḥuppah**, a wedding canopy. This is a symbol of the home which the couple are about to set up. Sometimes a ḥuppah is made by stretching a tallit between four poles. This emphasises the religious significance of the marriage. The Hebrew word for the wedding ceremony is **Kiddushin**. Like Kiddush, the blessing over wine, Kiddushin comes from a word meaning 'to make holy'.

Extended family

The family that a Jewish child belongs to is wider than just parents and brothers and sisters. There is also a very close relationship with grandparents and with aunts and uncles. But since the Holocaust − the Nazi persecution during the Second World War, when six million Jews were killed − many children have not been able to have the experience of belonging to a large family.

"My mother had two brothers. One was sent to a concentration camp and he didn't survive. The other escaped across Europe and Russia in cattle trucks, and he survived the rest of the war in China. My father's father was the only member of his family who came to this country. His brothers and sisters and their children and grandchildren were sent to concentration camps, and only a very few of them survived."

The local community

"I grew up in north-east London, where there was a big Jewish community. I didn't go to a Jewish school, but I did belong to a Jewish youth club, and I had lots of Jewish friends who had the same way of life as me."

In some cities, such as London and Leeds and Manchester, there are large Jewish communities, but Jews also live in many other towns and cities in Britain. Some of the people who have shared their experiences of growing up in Judaism for this book live in Cambridge, where the Orthodox community is quite small.

Being different

*"We took our son to Israel when he was three. When he saw all these men wearing **kippot** on their head, he went along saying it was a Jewish car, a Jewish lamp post, a Jewish cat! Everything! It was the contrast with Cambridge, for everyone there was Jewish."*

"Once Dad and some friends and I had a very nasty experience. We were walking to synagogue on Rosh Ha-Shanah, and we met a couple of skinheads − in their early twenties − who were disgusting. They were saying nasty things about the Holocaust − 'Gas ovens', 'Do you have gas at home?', 'Hitler', 'Kill the Jews!' and all that kind of thing. It makes me so angry. It may be my age. I just don't have the patience with it that older people do. They say, 'Well, never mind. So what? Big deal. Let them say it. Don't lower ourselves to their level.'"

Synagogues In cities where large numbers of Jewish people live, there will be many synagogues. Some will be Orthodox, where the traditional practices and forms of worship are continued, and some will be Reform. In Reform synagogues most of the service is in the language of the country (e.g. English or French or German), and men and women sit together. In traditional synagogues, almost all the service is in Hebrew, and the women sit separately from the men, often in a gallery.

> In Reform Judaism women can take part in the services. They can open the Aron Ha-kodesh, carry the Torah scrolls, lead the prayers and be called up to the reading of the Torah. And in recent times there have been a number of women rabbis.

In Orthodox synagogues girls under twelve and boys under thirteen ($\longrightarrow$ page 61) can choose whether they sit with the women or the men, and nobody minds if they go from one place to the other during the service. The atmosphere in an Orthodox synagogue is fairly relaxed. Observant Jews study the Torah and the Talmud as often as they can, and they say prayers three times a day, so the synagogue service on a Shabbat morning is not the only occasion in the week when they worship. The fact that the members of the community are together is also important.

Community centre *"Our children think of the synagogue not just as a place to pray, but also as a place where they meet friends. When we want to leave at the end of the service, we have to look for the children because all four have gone off and are talking to different people."*

The Hebrew for synagogue is **Bet Ha-Kenesset**, which means House of Meeting. As well as worshipping there, many young people and adults will meet there to study Torah and Talmud. Hebrew classes for children will be held there, and youth groups and perhaps women's groups and senior citizens will meet there. A synagogue is a real community centre.

"My mother was a refugee from Nazi Germany. When I said to her, 'What did you do when you were little?' all that she had done had been in Germany, and the Jewish community and everything which had been there was not there now for her to refer back to."

Hebrew classes for children are held at the synagogue.

The land of Israel

"Israel is always what I have felt most strongly about, in all of being Jewish. Maybe every Jew is born with this feeling of identity with the country. I don't know where it started. You grow up knowing about Israel, and you go to Israel. It's just so difficult living as a religious Jew in a non-religious atmosphere. Israel is an ideal to look towards, so that is why it's so wonderful that I can actually go and live there."

The State of Israel was created in 1948. There had always been some Jews living in the country, but the Jewish state had been destroyed by the Romans in 70 CE. Jews lived in many different countries, especially in Europe, but they often had to suffer persecution. When the worst persecution started — the Holocaust — many nations refused to allow Jews to come into their countries, so the creation of the State of Israel meant that Jews again had a country of their own.

Masada

"Masada means an awful lot to me, standing out defiantly. Those Zealots knew that there was no hope of winning against the Roman Empire, but they still took their stand. They all died for it. It's very symbolic. It makes you feel really proud of those Zealots. You almost wish you could have been there, in their shoes."

The story of the siege of Masada is very dramatic. In 70 CE, when Jerusalem was conquered, a large group of Zealots fled to the top of Masada. This is an enormous rock, at the southern end of the Dead Sea. It is more than a hundred metres high, and over nine hectares across the top. Herod the Great had earlier used it as his winter palace. The Tenth Legion of the Roman army built a wall right round the base of the rock and laid siege to it. For three years they were not able to subdue the Zealots. But then they built a great ramp of rubble, laced with beams of wood, against one side of the rock. They pushed their war engines up the ramp and catapulted burning objects over the walls to set the buildings on fire. When they eventually climbed over the walls they found that the Zealots were dead. They discovered two women and three children hiding in a cave, and learned from them that the Zealots had committed suicide. They had chosen to die rather than be taken by the Romans.

Masada is today a powerful symbol of resistance against an enemy power which is determined to destroy the Jewish state. New recruits to the Israeli army have a special ceremony on the top of Masada, and swear, 'Masada shall not fall again'.

Jerusalem

"Jerusalem is different from anywhere else because although it's a big city it's still definitely Jewish. Buses don't run on Shabbat. In other places they do. Tel Aviv is just like any other metropolitan city. Being in a big town, much bigger than Cambridge, and still having this overwhelmingly strong Judaism is something really special. But it's so frustrating not being able to go into the Temple area. It's our one piece of holy ground in the world."

Jerusalem is the 'centre' of Judaism. In a synagogue the Aron Ha-kodesh (⟶ page 19) is always set in the wall which faces Jerusalem. In biblical times Jews used to go to Jerusalem for the three pilgrim festivals (⟶ page 57). The most important one was Pesaḥ, and every year at the end of the Seder everyone says, 'L'shanah ha-ba'ah birushalayim' − 'Next year in Jerusalem'.

לְשָׁנָה הַבָּאָה בִּירוּשָׁלָיִם

In the Bible Jerusalem is called Zion, the City of David, the City of God. It has been a holy city to Jews ever since King David made it his capital and put the Ark of the Covenant there (2 Samuel 6:15). Then his son, Solomon, built the Temple in Jerusalem, to house the Ark of the Covenant. Jerusalem was the most sacred city for Jews and the Temple was the most sacred place of worship. All that is left of the Temple now is part of the outer wall which surrounded the Temple area. This is called the Western Wall.

As a result of the war which followed the establishment of the State of Israel in 1948, Jerusalem was divided between Israel and Jordan. The Temple area was in the Jordanian part of the city, so no Jew could go near the Western Wall. In 1967, after what is called the 'Six Day War', Israel gained control of the whole of Jerusalem, and the Western Wall has become a place of pilgrimage for Jews from all over the world. Many families go to Israel when their sons are about to turn thirteen, so that they can have their Bar Mitzvah ceremony at the Western Wall.

People of the Covenant

Circumcision

'Blessed are you, O Lord our God, King of the Universe, who has made us holy with your commands, and has commanded us to bring this boy into the Covenant of Abraham our father.'

That is the prayer that is spoken by the father at the circumcision of his son. **B'rit Milah** means 'Covenant of Circumcision', and it is a ritual which is performed on the eighth day after a boy's birth. It is based on God's command to Abraham ($\longrightarrow$ Genesis 17:9–12), and it is the sign, which all Jewish males carry, of belonging to God's Covenant.

Circumcision involves a very small operation – the removal of the foreskin. This is a religious rite rather than a medical one, so it is normally carried out by a **mohel**, a person who is highly skilled at performing the operation but who is also an observant Jew.

Naming

"Naming a baby isn't as big a thing in Judaism as it is with Christians. Of course a baby boy's name has to be registered when the birth is registered, but the religious part is when the mohel announces the baby's name at the B'rit Milah. And there is also a Jewish ceremony on the Shabbat after the birth, when the father is called up to the reading of the Torah."

A baby girl is usually named in the synagogue on the first Shabbat after her birth when the father is called up to the reading of the Torah. This is how she may be named:

'May he who blessed Sarah, Rebekah, Rachel and Leah ... Bless this beloved child, and may her name be _____.'

Covenant

The religion of Judaism is based on the covenant relationship between God and the Jewish people. Jews believe that God entered into this special relationship with their forefathers thousands of years ago, and gave them the Torah to show them how he wanted them to live.

The Covenant is not between God and *individual* Jews. The book of Exodus in the Bible describes how God made the Covenant with the whole Jewish people ($\longrightarrow$ Exodus 24:3–8). So there is a close relationship between all the people of the Covenant as well as between them and God.

Circumcision is the sign of belonging to the Covenant. It does not make a person a member of the Covenant, because anyone who has a Jewish mother is already Jewish, and everyone who is Jewish is a member of the Covenant people.

Charity

One of the ways in which children become aware that they belong to a very big 'family' is through **tzedakah**. This Hebrew word actually means 'doing the right thing' (doing what God wants you to do), and it refers to charity, giving to people in need.

"We have a box at home, and everyone in the family puts some money in every week, just before Shabbat. We did it from when we were really small. We gave part of our pocket money. Our box is for Jewish blind people."

Youth movements

Many children and young people go to Jewish youth clubs. These are often run by one of the youth movements.

*"The youth movement I belong to is Bnei Akiva. It has camps for different age groups, from about nine up to sixteen. After that you tend to become a leader and help with the younger children. At the end of the fifth form there is usually a trip to Israel, about six weeks. You work on a **kibbutz** for a while, and then you travel round the country, being shown round. Bnei Akiva encourages its members to have a year off after they leave school and go to Israel."*

"I go to camp every year. It's really good. You get to know loads of Jewish people. At the last camp there were 140 Jewish children from all over the place. I made some really good friends and I've kept in contact with them. We have great fun. We don't go to sleep for an hour or two after we are supposed to. There are really good games. And they tell you everyday laws about being Jewish. You can invite friends, even if they're not very religious. They can still go along and have fun, but we have prayers three times a day, so if you are not used to it, it can be a bit hard going."

"There is another Jewish boy in my class who is not so religious, and the thing that people in school find hard to understand is — how does he eat their meat and I don't, how does he come to school on Saturday and I don't. Since I'm more strict, sometimes they turn on him and say, 'You call yourself Jewish? You're just skiving. You're not really Jewish at all.' He has a hard time of it sometimes."

One of the ways in which children learn that in the Jewish community everyone belongs, no matter whether they are religious or not, is through the interpretation which the Rabbis gave to the four species which make up the lulav which is waved during the synagogue services at Sukkot (⟶ page 17):

Taste represents learning and smell represents good deeds.
    The palm has taste but no smell.
    The myrtle has smell but no taste.
    The etrog has both taste and smell.
    The willow has neither taste nor smell.

But all are bound together. So all Jewish people are bound together as people of the Covenant.

"Israel is very special to me because it is so multi-national and multi-racial, having Jews from countries as far apart as Ethiopia, England, Yemen, Morocco and the United States."

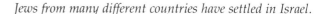
Jews from many different countries have settled in Israel.

Jews live in many countries in the world. Most of them are Ashkenazi. This is the name given to those who originally lived in Germany but who later migrated to Eastern European countries such as Poland. Many Askenazi Jews today live in Britain and America. Sephardi Jews originally lived in Spain and Portugal. There are some minor differences in the practices of Ashkenazi and Sephardi Jews. One of them is the Sephardic custom of keeping Torah scrolls in decorated metal containers that open outwards rather than in silk or velvet mantles.

> Jews who don't live in Israel are said to belong to the Diaspora, which means 'dispersed', 'scattered'.

Tradition

"One of the main attractions of Judaism for me is the continual tradition of history — the way this tradition has been handed down to us and the way it is being handed on to the children."

The Mosaic Covenant was made more than three thousand years ago, and Jews have a strong sense of being united with all the people of the Covenant down through history, not just with those who are alive today. There are many ways in which children come to realise that they belong to a religion with a very long history.

The three pilgrim festivals are reminders of the time when the Mosaic Covenant was made. Pesah celebrates the escape of the Hebrew slaves from Egypt and the beginning of their journey to Mount Sinai, where the Covenant was made. Shavuot celebrates the giving of the Decalogue, the Ten Commandments, at Mount Sinai. And at Sukkot Jews remember the way their ancestors had to live when they were journeying through the wilderness on their way from Egypt to the Promised Land.

When they study Talmud, the children of Orthodox families are actually entering into a kind of conversation with the great Jewish teachers of the past. Talmud study involves thinking about and discussing the teachings of Rabbis who lived in many different centuries ($\longrightarrow$ page 39).

The Temple

"The Western Wall has always had a lot of significance for me. Of course there's nothing special about a stone wall, only the feeling that the wall has stood there so long, and that Jews have been praying there. And priests, like my ancestors, hundreds of years ago walked past those walls with sacrifices. That's what I'd have been doing if I had been alive then. It's amazing to think about that."

The Temple at Jerusalem was destroyed in 70 CE, but there are many reminders of it in the religion today. The most important symbol of Judaism is the **Menorah**, the seven-branched candlestick. Children may see it on the mantle of a Sefer Torah, or on the curtain in front of the Aron Ha-kodesh, or on a synagogue building, or on Rosh Ha-Shanah cards ... There was a seven-branched candlestick in the Temple which King Solomon built nearly three thousand years ago. The Ner Tamid, the Eternal Light, that hangs in synagogues today is a reminder of the Temple menorah which was never allowed to go out.

The fast, Tisha B'Av (the ninth of Av), is a day of mourning for the destruction of Solomon's Temple by Nebuchadrezzar's Babylonian army in 586 BCE and the destruction of the Second Temple in 70 CE. Children are not involved in Tisha B'Av as much as they are in the festivals, but they will know that this is the saddest day of the Jewish year. They will see their father and older brothers praying without putting on their tallit or their tefillin, and when they notice this and ask about it, they will be told that it is a sign of mourning for the loss of the Temple.

Recent history

Jewish children learn about the people of the Covenant in more recent times as well as thousands of years ago. The festival of Yom Ha'atzmaut celebrates the creation in 1948 of a country that could be 'home' to every Jew who wants to go and live there. And at Yom Ha-Shoah children are very aware of the six million people of the Covenant who died in the Holocaust.

"When one is a young child one is told about the Holocaust, one knows what it was. I knew that six million Jews were killed. When there were films on TV Mum and Dad generally steered us clear of them. We were told it was better not to see those things; we'd get upset. We get upset when we see them now, but a little child would get upset without getting anything out of it."

Make a list of all the things which help Jewish children to be aware that they are members of the Covenant people.

Grown up!

"I suppose you could say that I started preparing for my Bar Mitzvah when I was two! The actual ceremony is what all your learning has been leading up to. When I was twelve I was first given an English translation of the passage I was going to read. Then we went through it in Hebrew, and then I studied what a famous scholar said about it."

Reading the Torah

"The Bar Mitzvah boy reads part or all of the portion of the Torah which is read in the synagogue on the Saturday morning. The Sefer Torah is written in Hebrew but without any vowels or punctuation or musical notes to show you how to sing it. It takes a lot of learning. You have to remember the vowels so that you can read the words properly, and the punctuation so that you know where the end of the sentence is, and the notes so that you can sing it. I was very nervous when I started reading it in front of all those people, but as I went on I got less nervous and more confident, and it was fine really."

This boy is reading a passage from the Torah at his Bar Mitzvah ceremony at the Western Wall. A boy reads a Torah passage publicly for the first time at his Bar Mitzvah ceremony.

Bar Mitzvah means 'Son of the Commandments'. A boy becomes Bar Mitzvah on the first Shabbat after his thirteenth birthday. It is a very important occasion for him. It is a recognition that he is now a 'grown-up' in Judaism. He can make up a **minyan**, that is the minimum number of ten adult male Jews needed in Orthodox Judaism for certain acts of public worship. And he can be called up to the reading of the Torah in synagogue services.

"The idea is to give the Bar Mitzvah boy a great time. He is the centre of attention. That has never been the case before and it will never be the case again in the whole of his life. The wedding is the bride's day really, so it's the only day when you have a simḥa to yourself. At the party after the service the Bar Mitzvah boy sits at the top table, which is fun. He makes a speech. I've still got mine, in my Bar Mitzvah file."

Tefillin

As a 'grown-up' in the religion, the boy is now expected to observe all the mitzvot. One mitzvah is the wearing of tefillin (→ Deuteronomy 6:6—8). The word 'tefillin' comes from the word **tefillah**, which means 'prayer', and the tefillin are worn during prayer except on Shabbat and other holy days.

"I had my tefillin, which were given to me by my grandfather, about a month before my Bar Mitzvah, so that I could practise putting them on. I was so excited I couldn't wait to put them on."

Each of the tefillin has a long leather strap attached to it. One of them is bound on the arm, with the box opposite the heart. It is put on the weaker arm, so a left handed person would wear it on his right arm. Different reasons are given for this practice. One reason given by Rabbis in the Talmud is that in Deuteronomy 6:8—9 the commands are to 'bind' and to 'write', so one binds with the same hand that one uses for writing. The strap is wound seven times between the elbow and the wrist, three times round the middle finger, around the fourth finger, and once round the hand. This makes the letter 'shin' on the hand, standing for Shaddai.
The other box is placed on the head, immediately above the space between the eyes. The strap is used to fasten the box but then it just hangs loosely; it is not bound in the same way as the strap on the arm.

Tefillin are small leather boxes, made from the skin of a kosher animal. Inside are four passages from the Bible, written on parchment by a sofer: Exodus 13: 1−10 and 13: 11−16 and Deuteronomy 6: 4−9 and 11: 13−21.

Think about the way tefillin are made, and the way they are worn, and write down as many things you can think of about them that are symbolic − pointers to important aspects of the religion.

Bat Mitzvah

"It's not quite as big as Bar Mitzvah. You make a speech at a party. I'm going to have my Bat Mitzvah soon, and I'm going to make a speech about modern women in Jewish history, like Hannah Senesh, and Sarah Aaronson and Anne Frank. Anne Frank died when she was sixteen. She was in Holland hiding from the Nazis, but she was found and sent to a concentration camp. Hannah Senesh parachuted behind enemy lines − she was very brave. Sarah Aaronson helped the British against the Turks in Palestine in 1917."

Bat Mitzvah − 'Daughter of the Commandments' − has been introduced in recent times. In Reform Judaism there is usually a ceremony in the synagogue service like the ceremony for Bar Mitzvah. In traditional Judaism the girl does not take part in the service or read from the Torah, but she has a party at which she makes a speech, just as the boy does, and she may take part in a group ceremony after the service. A girl becomes Bat Mitzvah after her twelfth birthday, not her thirteenth, because girls mature earlier than boys.

Endings and beginnings

Bar Mitzvah and Bat Mitzvah mark a young person's entry into adult status in the religion. They now take on the adult responsibility of observing the mitzvot. They are still young, and there is lots more for them to learn. If they are observant Jews they will go on studying for the rest of their lives, but as far as their religion is concerned, they are now 'grown up'.

What do you think are the advantages and the difficulties of being regarded as grown up at twelve or thirteen?

Glossary

NB Words in quotation marks are the translation of the Hebrew words.
Pronunciation: The stress usually falls on the end of Hebrew words. When it falls on a different syllable this is indicated by an acute accent (´).

adonai 'lord'

afikoman piece of matzah hidden during Pesah meal

aliyah 'ascent', being called up to the reading of the Torah

amidah 'standing', name of important Jewish prayer

aron ha-kódesh the holy ark in the synagogue

berakhot 'blessings'

bet ha-knésset 'house of meeting', synagogue

bimah raised platform in the synagogue

b'rit milah 'covenant of circumcision'

dáven (Yiddish) 'to pray'

dreidl (Yiddish) four-sided top

gemara 'completion', commentaries on the Mishnah, part of the Talmud

haftarot readings from the Nevi'im in the synagogue service

hag, hagim 'festival(s)'

haggadah, haggadot 'narrative', 'telling', book(s) used at the Seder

halakhah 'walking', God's laws

hallah, hallot bread, loaves

hallel 'praise'

hametz leavened food

ha-motzi blessing over bread

hanukkiyah nine-branched candlestick (eight plus one)

havdalah 'separation', ceremony at end of Shabbat

huppah wedding canopy

kashrut food laws

ketuvim writings, section of the Bible

kibbutz Israeli settlement where work and possessions are shared

kiddush 'making holy', blessing over wine

kiddushin wedding ceremony

kippah, kippot skullcap(s)

kosher (anglicised form of **kasher**) 'fit', 'proper', permitted foods

lulav 'branch', palm branch used for the four species waved at Sukkot

magen david 'shield of David', the six-pointed star of David

matzah, matzot unleavened bread

megillah scroll of the book of Esther

menorah candlestick

mezuzah 'doorpost', parchment in small box fixed on doorpost

minyan minimum of ten adult Jews needed for public worship

mishnah collection of teachings of early rabbis, part of the Talmud

mitzvah, mitzvot 'commandment(s)'

mohel person who carries out ritual circumcision

ner tamid everlasting light

nevi'im 'prophets', second section of the Bible

páreve (Yiddish) food that is neither milk nor meat

rosh 'head'

séder 'order', celebration on first night of Pesaḥ

séfer, sifrei 'book(s)'

shaddai 'almighty'

shalom 'peace'

shammash 'servant', candle used to light the other eight candles in a hanukkiyah

shanah 'year'

shema 'hear', central Jewish prayer

shiur traditional study group

shofar ram's horn trumpet

shul (Yiddish) synagogue

siddur prayer book

simḥa 'celebration'

sofer 'scribe'

sukkah, sukkot 'booth(s)', 'tabernacle(s)'

tallit prayer shawl

tallit katan small prayer shawl, tzitzit

tanakh Bible: Torah, Nevi'im and Ketuvim

tefillah 'prayer'

tefillin leather boxes with straps worn for prayer, phylacteries

torah 'teaching', 'law', also the five books of Moses

tov, tovah 'good'

tref (Yiddish) foods that are forbidden

tzedakah 'righteousness', 'justice', charity

yad 'hand', pointer used in reading Torah Scroll

yarmulka (Yiddish) skullcap

yom 'day'

zemirah, zemirot Shabbat song(s)

Index

NB Words in the index refer to pages where the topic is discussed, and not only to those where the actual words occur.